I AM
a Daughter
of the Most High
King

30 Daily Declarations for Women

BABBIE MASON

Abingdon Press
Nashville

I Am a Daughter of the Most High King
30 Daily Declarations for Women

Copyright © 2016 Abingdon Press. All rights reserved.

This book is printed on elemental chlorine-free paper.

Library of Congress Cataloging--in--Publication Data
Names: Mason, Babbie, author.
Title: I am a daughter of the most high King : 30 daily declarations for
    women / Babbie Mason.
Description: First [edition]. | Nashville, Tennessee : Abingdon Press, 2016.
Identifiers: LCCN 2016001890 (print) | LCCN 2016002513 (ebook) | ISBN
    9781501813542 (pbk.) | ISBN 9781501815003 (e-book)
Subjects: LCSH: Christian women--Religious life. | Christian women--Prayers
    and devotions. | Affirmations--Miscellanea.
Classification: LCC BV4527 .M2684 2016 (print) | LCC BV4527 (ebook) | DDC
    242/.643--dc23
LC record available at http://lccn.loc.gov/2016001890

16 17 18 19 20 21 22 23 24 25 — 10 9 8 7 6 5 4 3 2 1
MANUFACTURED IN THE UNITED STATES OF AMERICA

In memory of my beloved mother,
Georgia Mae Stephen-Wade

October 4, 1923 – August 27, 2015

CONTENTS

My Authority: What I Can Do Through Christ

My Possibility: How I Can Face Each Day with Christ

Introduction

For more than three decades, I've been encouraging women at concerts, speaking to them at conferences, and teaching them in Bible studies. In my travels around the world, I have the joy of meeting women of all ages, races, cultures, and circumstances. I find we have more things in common than we have differences. We can all use a good laugh every now and then. We enjoy the warm embrace of a good friend. We need to be heard and understood. And most of all, we need to be loved and encouraged in our faith in Christ. I'm sure you can identify with those things just as much as I do.

Besides being with my own family, I love nothing more than being in a room full of girlfriends, encouraging them and telling them about Jesus. That's why I wrote this book of devotions, *I Am a Daughter of the Most High King*. Each page delivers a daily portion of fresh insight, heaps of hope, and loads of affirmation, helping you understand more fully your identity as God's beloved daughter. As you turn each page, I pray that you will sense the voice of God reminding you that you are deeply loved. He has a plan for you, and it is good. There is a place for you in God's forever family. And because of Jesus, you are worth it.

Over the course of the next thirty days, you will learn more about your royal relationship with your King and develop a better understanding of His love for you. You will be challenged to apply the words from the Bible—His love letter to you—to become the mature woman in Christ you are meant to be.

Starting today, I encourage you to find a quiet place where you can read one devotion a day for thirty days. Each devotion begins with a statement from The Declaration, a collection of faith-filled statements I've written, and follows with Scripture promises to uplift your heart and a challenge to call you to action. Each entry closes with a section called My Proclamation. Consider reading the proclamation aloud, with your heart, mind, and hands open to God. Then pray the prayer that follows, positioning yourself to receive from the Lord. Feel free to pray in your own words as well, because prayer is a two-way conversation with God. I would also encourage you to keep a journal nearby to capture what God is speaking to your heart.

Whether your devotional practice is the first thing you do each morning or the last thing you do after a hectic day, my prayer is that reading *I Am a Daughter of the Most High King* will help you establish time alone with God. Through that time, the most important time of the day, I pray you will be moved to a more intimate relationship with the Lord and enjoy being in His presence as you spend precious time with Him.

May you live as the royal daughter you are for the rest of your life!

Babbie Mason

The Declaration

I Am a Daughter of the Most High King

1. I am a daughter of the Most High King.
2. I am deeply loved, highly favored, and greatly blessed.
3. My identity is in Christ alone.
4. I know who I am and Whose I am.
5. I am the righteousness of God in Christ, accepted in the Beloved, a joint heir together with Christ, and part of the family of God.
6. I have decided to follow Jesus with all my heart.
7. There will be no turning around, no slacking up, no backing down, no striking out, and no giving in.
8. I will not compromise my faith, abandon my convictions, or cower in the face of adversity.
9. My past is forgiven.
10. My present has purpose.
11. My best and brightest days are still ahead of me.
12. I walk by faith and not by sight.
13. My gaze is fixed and my mind is made up.
14. I am determined not to think like the world, walk like the world, talk like the world, or act like the world.
15. I will not be moved.

16. I cannot be shaken.
17. I will not be swayed.
18. I belong to Jesus, and I set my sights on things above.
19. Earth is my mission, and heaven is my destiny.
20. I declare that "I can do all things through Christ who strengthens me" (Philippians 4:13 NKJV).
21. All things are possible. So if God is for me, who can be against me?
22. My faith is rooted and established in love.
23. Nothing I have done, or ever will do, can diminish God's power that is working in me and for me.
24. I have the mind of Christ on every matter. I make sound decisions, and I exercise good judgment.
25. I put my trust in God, regardless of what comes against me.
26. And nothing will be able to separate me from the love of God in Christ Jesus our Lord.
27. I eagerly await Christ's return.
28. On that great day He will know me and call me by name.
29. His banner over me is love.
30. And I lift my voice in loudest hallelujahs to sing His praises forevermore.

My Identity:
Who I Am in Christ

Day 1

The King's Daughter

I am a daughter of the Most High King.

Thou art worthy, O Lord, to receive glory and
honour and power: for thou hast created all things,
and for thy pleasure they are and were created.
(Revelation 4:11)

Do you know why you were created? God did not create you to be a success in the world's eyes or to create a name for yourself. Revelation 4:11 tells us that we were created to glorify God, to fellowship with Him, and to bring Him pleasure. Your relationship with God is what gives you worth and value. When you begin to understand that God loves you and has a plan for your life, you will begin to understand how precious you really are.

You were created on purpose, with a purpose, and for a purpose. You are not a mistake. You are not an irritation or an aggravation. God is not mad at you. You are not a burden or a nuisance to Him. You may have been a surprise to some, but you have never been a surprise to God. Psalm 139:16 says, "You saw me before I was born. / Every day of my life was recorded in your book. / Every moment was laid out / before a single day had passed" (NLT). The moment you discover that your true purpose is to glorify God with your life will be the moment you truly begin to live.

Today is the day to stop settling for less than your full potential. You don't need to *do* more. Jesus did it all so that you could *be* complete. Stop searching for validation from others. Because of Jesus, your purpose is established and you are already approved. You are your heavenly Father's daughter! How do we know this? God's Word says so! "See how very much our Father loves us, for he calls us his children, and that is what we are!" (1 John 3:1a NLT). Yes, that is who you truly are!

My Proclamation: Today I cease my striving, trying to do and be more. Instead, I rest in what Christ has already done. I celebrate the truth that God created me on purpose to bring Him glory. He is my King, and that makes me a member of His royal family.

Heavenly Father, thank You for creating me and giving me purpose in life. Forgive me for seeking significance elsewhere instead of finding my worth in You. Today I stop trying to earn what Jesus died to give me and I celebrate my relationship in You. In Jesus' name, Amen.

Day 2

Deeply Loved

I am deeply loved, highly favored, and greatly blessed.

For God so loved the world, that he gave his only begotten Son, that whosoever believeth in him should not perish, but have everlasting life. (John 3:16)

Have you ever considered how much God loves you? God not only loved the world, but He also loved you so passionately that He gave His dearest possession, the life of His own Son, for you.

John 3:16 is one of the most memorized Scripture verses, and many have been able to recite it by rote since childhood. Because it is so familiar, it has lost its impact to some. But the truth of the passage has not diminished. Deliberately read the words aloud: "For God so loved the world, that He gave His only begotten Son...." It's mind-boggling, but God loves you just as passionately as He loves His only Son, Jesus. God loves you as if you were the only one to love. He doesn't just love you in the way that our culture loosely defines love. God loves you unconditionally, sacrificially, and completely. As a matter of fact, He *so* loves you. The word *so* is defined as "to a great degree: very or extremely."[1] Jesus demonstrated how far His love would go when He was hung high—arms stretched wide on the cross—saying to the whole world, "I love you this much."

Because God deeply loves you, He desires to smile on you, to show His generous kindness toward you. He delights in being good to you—in blessing you. This tremendous kindness is called *favor*. Finding God's favor gives you the assurance that He is always with you and has your best interests at heart. In response to God's undeserved favor, your humble and wise response is to take great care to live a life that is pleasing to Him. Proverbs 8:35 says, "For those who find me [wisdom] find life / and receive favor from the Lord" (NIV).

Read John 3:16 again, this time replacing the word *whosoever* and all the other pronouns in the passage with your name. Remind yourself that you are deeply loved, highly favored, and greatly blessed. May you never take those promises for granted but allow them to draw you closer to your heavenly Father's heart.

My Proclamation: I find confidence in the promise that God loves me as if I were the only one to love. Developing an intimate relationship with Jesus, my Savior, is my highest priority.

Dear Father, I am overwhelmed by how much You love me. Thank You for caring for me the way You do. Help me never to take this powerful truth for granted. In Jesus' name, Amen.

It's mind-boggling,
but God loves you just as passionately
as He loves His only Son, Jesus.

Day 3

In Christ Alone

My identity is in Christ alone.

But you are a chosen generation, a royal priesthood, a holy nation, His own special people, that you may proclaim the praises of Him who called you out of darkness into His marvelous light.

(1 Peter 2:9 NKJV)

Do you know that your identity is not defined by what you do, your relationship to others, or what others say about you? Your identity is defined by who God says you are. In order for you to live the life God has designed for you, you must agree wholeheartedly with what God says about you in His Word. God's opinion of you is the only opinion that matters. God created you. He knows the real you, and He wants you to know the real you, too.

Your heavenly Father finds great joy in loving you. It breaks His heart when His children look for love in all the wrong places or resist His love. It grieves Him when you don't believe that He loves you and desires to bless you. Thinking like this is choosing not to believe what God has said in His Word or the work that Jesus did on the cross.

Each time you look into a mirror today, remind yourself that you are chosen, royal, holy, and special. You are valuable because you belong to God. Reread today's verse, 1 Peter 2:9. God's Word says you are chosen. This means you are selected, handpicked by God. You are part of a royal priesthood. You are royal because your Father is a King! You are a priest who goes before the Father to intercede for others. You are God's beautiful representation of Himself in the earth. You are holy and set apart— a priceless treasure.

God made you a part of His forever family. Before God chose to make the universe, He chose you. Ephesians 1:4 says, "Even before he made the world, God loved us and chose us in Christ to be holy and without fault in his eyes" (NLT). You are valuable because you belong to God.

My Proclamation: Today I agree with what God's Word says about me. Regardless of what others have spoken to me or about me, I find my identity in Christ Jesus. I am chosen, royal, holy, and special. I am valuable because I belong to God.

Heavenly Father, thank You for the promises of Your Word. Your Word changes everything, including me! Hurtful words were spoken over me concerning my identity. Some go back as far as my childhood. But I believe You are healing my heart now. I agree with who You say I am now, and that settles it. In Jesus' name, Amen.

Day 4

You Belong

I know who I am and Whose I am.

Being confident of this, that he who began a good work in you will carry it on to completion until the day of Christ Jesus. (Philippians 1:6 NIV)

What you do is not who you are. I am a singer and a songwriter by vocation. But if I never sing another note or write another song, I am still complete and loved by God. When you allow what you do to establish your identity, you'll always believe you must compete with others to be considered successful.

Who you are is not what you have accomplished. When you are defined by your accomplishments, you'll find yourself trying to measure up in order to be accepted, which always leads to disappointment.

Who you are is not what others have said about you. If you allow yourself to be defined by others, you will value their opinions much too highly and become a people-pleaser. Been there. Done that.

None of these things can define your true identity. Only God has that privilege.

Philippians 1:6 begins with two definitive words: *being confident*. This tells us that we can find complete trust in the fact that God always finishes what He starts. The work He started in you long before you were born is being perfected in you day by day. So don't allow fickle feelings or insecure people to dictate how you should live. Instead, agree with God's Word.

The enemy of your soul does not want you to discover your true identity. He has one mission: to steal your joy, kill your dreams, and destroy your hopes (see John 10:10). Put your foot down and your hand up and tell him this is where you draw the line. You are God's property.

Use God's Word as your weapon and take your identity back today. Live your life according to your heavenly Father's promises for you. Determine that you will not stand in the way of the work God wants to do in your life.

My Proclamation: Today I celebrate who and Whose I am. I walk out God's plan for me without apology. I belong to Him, and I am confident that He will finish the work He started in me. I look to Him only to complete me and reveal my true identity.

Heavenly Father, forgive me for looking to others to validate my identity. That stops today. Thank You that Your Word is the hedge of protection I need to protect my heart and mind from the plot of the enemy. I look only to You now, and I see myself in the reflection of Your Word. In Jesus' name, Amen.

Because Jesus gave His life for you,
you have all the rights and privileges
as Jesus Himself.

Day 5

Adopted and Accepted

I am the righteousness of God in Christ, accepted in the Beloved, a joint heir together with Christ, and a part of the family of God.

Even before he made the world, God loved us and chose us in Christ to be holy and without fault in his eyes. God decided in advance to adopt us into his own family by bringing us to himself through Jesus Christ. This is what he wanted to do, and it gave him great pleasure. So we praise God for the glorious grace he has poured out on us who belong to his dear Son. (Ephesians 1:4-6 NLT)

Did you know that you are adopted? You have been embraced as a daughter into God's family. You are accepted, approved by God's unconditional love through Jesus Christ. And you have been made acceptable, pleasing to God. You bring Him great pleasure and delight. You are enough because Jesus is enough. Because Jesus gave His life for you, you have all the rights and privileges as Jesus Himself. You are a daughter of the Most High King, a rightful heir to every blessing in your heavenly Father's kingdom.

So don't wallow in the guilt and shame of the past. If the past was significant to God, His name would be I Was. Don't worry about tomorrow and all of its unanswered questions. If the future was a concern to God, His name would be I WILL BE. Instead, bask in the promises of the present. Live in the moment, for "This *is* the day the LORD has made" (Psalm 118:24a NKJV). That's why He is called I AM. Rejoice and be glad that you are adopted, accepted, and acceptable—all because of what Jesus has done for you.

My Proclamation: Today I live in the present promise that I am the righteousness of God in Christ Jesus. I look at my past through the cross and my future through the Resurrection. I live in the moment by the grace of God. I am adopted, accepted, and acceptable to my heavenly King. Because of Jesus, I have a place to belong.

Dear Father God, finally I know where I belong! I have struggled with this for such a long time, trying to fit in with this group and that clique. Laboring to find acceptance is not Your plan for me. Now that I have found my place in Your Family, my heart is at peace. You love me just as I am, and with Your help I will grow to be the mature daughter You already see me to be. In Jesus' name, Amen.

Day 6

An Ambassador for Christ

I have decided to follow Jesus
with all my heart.

So we are Christ's ambassadors; God is making his
appeal through us. We speak for Christ when we
plead, "Come back to God!"
(2 Corinthians 5:20 NLT)

Have you ever said, "My life doesn't make a difference. What can one person do?" But just think about the profound difference that individual believers have made throughout the ages—from the great heroes of faith mentioned in Hebrews 11 to the countless unknown and unrecorded persons of faith whose contributions and influence can never be measured.

Recently I've heard people say, "There's so much trouble in the world; somebody should do something." God *did* do something. He created you! It doesn't matter how big or small your efforts are; God sees them as a sacrifice that makes an eternal impact on others. There's a saying popularly attributed to Mother Teresa: "Never worry about numbers. Help one person at a time, and always start with the person nearest you."[2] We can take time from our busy schedules to become actively involved in the welfare of our neighbor. We can show concern. We can speak kind words. We can commit our resources. We can "go" or we can "send" someone else. Doing what you can, while seasoning your actions with the love of Christ, is the greatest gift of all.

Today, sing a chorus of the hymn "I Have Decided to Follow Jesus" to express your commitment to Christ. If you don't know the hymn, search for it on the Internet. As you sing, be reminded of the sacrifice others have made so that you could hear the gospel of Jesus Christ. In a response of gratitude, find some way to spread the love of Christ in the world where you live.

My Proclamation: I am an ambassador of Christ. His love in me is on display as I represent Him at home, in the marketplace, and beyond. Wherever I go, the love of Christ goes with me, and I make myself available to be used by Him today.

Dear Father, You have quickened my heart today and reminded me of the importance of sharing my faith. Only people place a measure on how great or small an effort is. You, on the other hand, have shown me that even "little things" carry a lot of weight in Your economy. Help me in some small way to make a big difference in someone's life today as I spread Your love. I will be sure to give Your name glory. In Jesus' name, Amen.

It doesn't matter how big or small your efforts are; God sees them as a sacrifice that makes an eternal impact on others.

Day 7

Encourage Yourself

**There will be no turning around,
no slacking up, no backing down,
no striking out, and no giving in.**

But David encouraged himself in the LORD His God.
(1 Samuel 30:6)

You may read today's declaration and say, "That's easier to say than do!" Maybe you don't have enough resources, and it's only the middle of the month. Maybe you're a single mom and you find yourself tossing and turning at night with worry concerning your teenager. It's a real challenge going through these tough years alone. It could be that your marriage has hit a tough spot. The wedding vows were beautiful on the day of the ceremony but now it's a struggle to stay when those vows are broken. Don't quit! There is encouragement for you in the middle of your challenge.

First Samuel 30:1-6 tells how David and his troops came home to Ziklag only to find that everything they treasured had been wiped out. The Amalekites had raided the town, setting it on fire. Then they took the women and children as their prisoners. When David and his soldiers returned to this devastation, these mighty men wept until they had no more tears.

The word *discouragement* doesn't begin to describe the condition of David's heart and those of his men. David's troops even threatened to stone him in the middle of this horrendous ordeal. In the midst of the despair, "David encouraged himself in the LORD his God." David did for himself what no one else could do.

Are you discouraged by burdens that weigh heavily on your heart? The key to victory is found in the words you speak. You can bring yourself down by speaking negative words. Or you can let your own words pull you up. Instead of using negative words to complain about your circumstances, use uplifting words to change your outlook. Go into your prayer closet and ask God to help you see things from His point of view. Then, when you come out, you will emerge stronger, remembering that no one can encourage you the way that you can encourage yourself.

My Proclamation: Today I will not negate my faith by speaking words of discouragement concerning my circumstances. In speaking words that lift up, I build up my faith, encouraging myself in the Lord.

Awesome Father, I have spoken words that have actually made my circumstances worse, not better. Forgive me for contributing to my own problem. Put Your words in my mouth and Your song in my heart. In Your Word I find the strength I need. In Jesus' name, Amen.

My Security:

What I Have

Because of Christ

Day 8

Standing Up for God

I will not compromise my faith, abandon my convictions, or cower in the face of adversity.

Then the other administrators and high officers began searching for some fault in the way Daniel was handling government affairs, but they couldn't find anything to criticize or condemn. He was faithful, always responsible, and completely trustworthy.
(Daniel 6:4 NLT)

Every woman feels the need to belong and be accepted by her peers. But sometimes when you stand for God, you have to stand alone. The Bible tells of a man with noble character, Daniel, who found favor with God because he would not compromise his faith.

King Darius was so impressed with Daniel's integrity, ability, and dedication that he placed Daniel over the affairs of the whole kingdom of Babylon. The Bible says that the other officials were so jealous of Daniel's promotion that they tried to dig up dirt concerning Daniel's character (Daniel 6:4 -5). When they couldn't find anything, these evil men conspired and convinced the king to issue an edict saying that anyone who prayed to any god or man, except the king, would be killed. When Daniel decided to disobey the king's law rather than dishonor his God, he was thrown into a hungry lions' den. But the next morning, Daniel miraculously came out without so much as a scratch on him. God had protected His faithful follower.

So what is the message for God's daughter today? The virtues of honor, character, and courage are not just for Old Testament prophets. God is looking all over the earth to find a woman whose heart is upright before Him. God is looking for you. He wants you to uphold His standard of righteousness and declare that there are some things you just won't do. There are places you refuse to go, with people you refuse to call friends. When truth is on the line, you must place a higher priority on serving God than the opinions of the world. God will help you do this. He provides a refuge for those who trust in Him.

My Proclamation: I declare that I am a bold witness for God. I do not permit compromise to weaken my faith. I hold fast to my convictions because I fear God and obey Him.

Father, my relationship with You is far more important than anything else. I want to be found upright and honorable in Your eyes. When I feel pressure to disobey You, give me strength to stand for what is right. Give me the words to speak up when given the opportunity. I want to do this because I know it pleases You. In Jesus' name, Amen.

Because of Jesus, your past is in the past. No matter what you have done, Jesus wiped your slate clean and gave you a brand-new start.

Day 9

A Brand-New Start

My past is forgiven.

Now we look inside, and what we see is that anyone united with the Messiah gets a fresh start, is created new. The old life is gone; a new life burgeons!
(2 Corinthians 5:17 The Message)

The teenage girl stood before the judge with great apprehension. She would have to pay a high price for her mistakes—her driver's license would be revoked, she would have to pay fines, and she would have to spend time in jail. Before being taken away to begin serving her sentence, the judge asked if she understood what it meant to be found guilty. The teenager quietly acknowledged that she understood. The judge asked her if she knew the damage she had caused by committing the crime. Again, the young lady affirmed that she understood. Then the judge spoke words that would change the young lady's life: "If you do all that is required of you, I will remove this conviction from your record on your eighteenth birthday. It will be as if you never did anything wrong." The weight of the world was lifted from the teenager's shoulders, and she began to feel free.

Disobedience to God is called *sin*. We can try to excuse our sinful behavior by saying things like, "Everybody else was doing it. I just caved in." We can try to blame others by saying something like, "I am this way because of my parents' divorce." We can even try to get on God's good side by doing good deeds to relieve our guilt. But none of that works. The guilty feelings always return.

The reason you feel guilty is because *you are.* But there is good news! You are not the only person who is guilty of sin. Everyone in the whole world has sinned (see Romans 3:23). When Jesus died on the cross, your sins were forgiven and you were set free of guilt and shame. Because of Jesus, your past is in the past. No matter what you have done, Jesus wiped your slate clean and gave you a brand-new start. He forgives you. What's next? Forgive yourself.

My Proclamation: With a heart of gratitude, I boldly confess that I am forgiven of sin. I am relieved of guilt, and I no longer carry the burden of shame connected to it. Because of Jesus, I am free and my past is forgiven.

Dear Father, thank You for forgiving my past mistakes and granting me a brand-new start. I have the assurance that my past is in the past and the burdens of guilt and shame are lifted. In Jesus' name, Amen.

Day 10

Finding Purpose in the Pain

My present has purpose.

*When the woman saw that she was not hid, she
came trembling and falling down before him, she
declared unto him before all the people for what
cause she had touched him, and how she was healed
immediately. And [Jesus] said unto her, Daughter, be
of good comfort: thy faith hath made thee whole; go
in peace. (Luke 8:47-48)*

Are you dealing with an issue that seems out of your
control, one that overwhelms you and drains you of
money, health, or peace of mind? One woman in the
Bible knew that experience all too well. She had depleted
her finances trying to find a solution for her sickness, but
after twelve long years, she was no better off than when
she began. According to Mosaic law, this suffering woman
with an "issue of blood" was considered unclean, an
outcast. She likely lived outside the city walls, away from
the general population. She would not know the joy of
intimate friendships or family gatherings. Her life was one
of isolation and loneliness. But this woman did not give up.

Word had spread that Jesus could heal the sick, raise
the dead, and cast out evil spirits. It must have taken real

courage for her to leave home and navigate the streets to find Jesus, but she did not let the opportunity pass her by. Weak, anemic, and afraid, she dared to reach out and touch the hem of His garment as He passed by.

Don't you love how Jesus responded to her? He did not reprimand her for touching Him or publically embarrass her for touching others. He didn't criticize her for breaking religious laws. Instead, He validated her and called her *daughter*, a term of deep love and concern. Jesus knew her need, just as surely as He had felt her desperate touch.

Jesus brings purpose to pain. He masterfully heals wounded hearts. He rebuilds broken lives. He restores dysfunctional families. And He breathes new life back into dashed dreams that are well on their way to the trash heap. Don't let your challenges define you—instead, let them lead you to Jesus.

My Proclamation: Today I boldly confess that I am an overcomer and a victor over my issues. My challenges only bring out the best in me. I take refuge in the fact that the Lord is my very present help in a time of trouble.

Precious Father, I find great comfort in knowing that You care about the issues I face today. Of all the relationships I have, the one I treasure most is the friendship I share with You. You truly make life worth living. In Jesus' name, Amen.

Day 11

Be the Blessing

My best and brightest days
are still ahead of me.

*Give, and you will receive. Your gift will return to
you in full—pressed down, shaken together to make
room for more, running over, and poured into your
lap. The amount you give will determine the amount
you get back. (Luke 6:38 NLT)*

It was an exciting day. My friend had just produced
her first motion picture, and on the way to the premiere, I
decided that I should bring a gift. The only nearby store was
one of those big warehouse-type superstores, so I dashed
in to grab a nice gift and a bouquet of flowers. Standing in
the checkout line, I realized that in order to purchase the
items I'd need a membership card, which I didn't have. A
very nice woman in line offered to let me use hers. With
gratitude I replied, "Oh, thank you so much! God bless
you for that!"

"Oh, honey," she said, "I really do need God to bless
me. I've had a tough go of it these last few months. My
grandkids have come to live with me, and I'm not as young
as I used to be." In an effort to encourage her, I smiled and
said, rather conversationally, "Well, I pray that God will

open up the windows of His heaven and shower down so many blessings upon you and your grandchildren that you won't have room to receive them all." Before I could get the words out of my mouth she was lifting her hands and shouting praises to God, right there in the checkout line.

Before I could turn around, a young woman in line asked for a blessing too, so while the first lady was yet praising God, I smiled, took the young woman by the hand, and spoke a promise from God's Word as tears rolled down her face. That was the first time I'd ever had church in the checkout line of a warehouse superstore!

The words I spoke to those I met at the store weren't unusual—I only did what God led me to do in that moment. How is He leading you to bless someone in your path today?

My Proclamation: Today I am the blessing that someone needs. As I give myself away to others, blessings will come back to me in good measure, pressed down, shaken together, running over, making room for more.

Loving Father, love others through me today. Put me in the right places to share Your love. Allow me the privilege to bring out the best in others, and allow them to see that You are loving, kind, and good. I know this brings joy to Your heart, as it certainly brings joy to mine! In Jesus' name, Amen.

Day 12

Faith Over Feelings

I walk by faith and not by sight.

For we walk by faith, not by sight.
(2 Corinthians 5:7)

Do you have a tendency to obsess over the unanswered questions of life? Are you wringing your hands with worry over how a recent health diagnosis could play out? Do you wonder how your college-aged child may be doing while away at school? Too often, we speculate and even play out imaginary scenarios in our minds about things that may never happen.

The heart of your intimate relationship with God is summed up in one simple word: *faith*. Believing that faith needs no explanation, determine to anchor yourself in His Word and leave the outcome to Him. No matter what your situation looks like, determine that you will not waver in relying on God. It's easy to let our feelings get in the way, but with God's help, you can sidestep your emotions by basing your feelings on facts, not your facts on feelings. You can *be* confident without *feeling* confident. You can fall flat on your face and still find confidence in God to get up and try again. You can make poor choices, and by God's grace, still end up on the right road. Why? Your confidence does not come as a result of your accomplishments; your confidence comes by realizing God's power is greater than your need.

The Bible is full of amazing accounts in which God instructed people to step outside of traditional wisdom to put their faith in God. The Lord spoke to the tribe of Judah, telling them to march into the battle singing victory songs instead of fighting their enemies with traditional weapons (2 Chronicles 20:21). Jesus told Peter to get out of the boat to walk on water (Matthew 14:29). And Jesus told His disciples to feed a multitude of more than five thousand people with only two fish and five loaves (Matthew 14:13-21).

When God leads, will the details be sketchy sometimes? Absolutely! Will walking by faith always make sense? No. But not to worry. Remarkable things happen when we walk by faith and not by feelings.

My Proclamation: Today, I unapologetically declare that I trust God's Word, regardless of how I feel. If God's Word says it, I believe it. I anchor myself in God's Word, leaving the outcome to Him.

Dear Heavenly Father, I admit I sometimes find it difficult to walk by faith. But I know deep in my heart that You will never take me down a path that has no purpose. Help me to let You lead as I learn to follow in the footsteps of faith. In Jesus' name, Amen.

*Your confidence does not come as a
result of your accomplishments;
your confidence comes by realizing
God's power is greater than your need.*

Day 13

Just Keep Marching

My gaze is fixed and my mind is made up.

*Have not I commanded thee? Be strong and of good
courage; be not afraid, neither be thou dismayed: for
the LORD thy God is with thee whithersoever thou
goest. (Joshua 1:9)*

After forty years of wandering in the desert, God
instructed Joshua to take His people into the Promised
Land. One thing stood in the way—overtaking the
fortressed city of Jericho.

Although it was an unconventional plan, God gave
Joshua concise instructions to bring the city of Jericho
crumbling to its knees. For six days, God instructed
Joshua and the Israelites to simply march around the
city of Jericho once a day. The Canaanites in the city
heckled and mocked God's people, but Joshua instructed
the Israelites to be silent—no second guessing or talking
back was permitted. On day seven, God told His people
to march around Jericho seven consecutive times. At the
appointed time, the priests blew their trumpets and the
people lifted their voices in a mighty shout of victory. The
walls of Jericho tumbled down, and the people of God
rushed in to capture the city. (See Joshua 6:20.)

God supernaturally reduced a formidable city to a heap of rubble, and the story of the battle of Jericho gives us three lessons to consider.

Don't talk back. Make up your mind to do things God's way. When God gives you His clear and concise instructions, don't murmur or vacillate. Listen to God and obey His commands, being careful not to take matters into your own hands.

Don't lay back. God's way may seem unconventional, but don't give up! Obey God with dogged determination, even when setbacks come or the plan doesn't make sense to you.

Don't turn back. Joshua knew what he was up against, but for the believer who desires to do God's will, retreating is never an option. Put on your boots and march!

Would you agree that it's time not only to *believe in* God, but to *believe* God and take Him at His word?

My Proclamation: I humbly submit to God's unique battle plan. I envision my promised land, although I may be staring at the walls of my Jericho. As a daughter of the Most High King, I know God is fighting for me and those walls must come down!

Strong Father, I know it's just a matter of time until the promise You have given me is fulfilled. Please, Lord, give me courage not to sabotage the process, but to obey, even in the face of challenge. With You on my side, victory is a sure thing! Thank You, God! In Jesus' name, Amen.

Day 14

It's Your Serve

I am determined not to think like the world, walk like the world, talk like the world, or act like the world.

Before I made you in your mother's womb, I chose you. / Before you were born, I set you apart for a special work. (Jeremiah 1:5 NCV)

If I peeked in your kitchen cupboard, I expect I'd find some "everyday" dishes—the ones you use to serve meals and snacks to your family. If I looked harder, I might also find a set of lovely china stored away in a special cupboard somewhere, rarely used except for special occasions. While the china may be more impressive in appearance, it is the everyday dishes—the sturdy ones with the nicks and scratches—that are regularly used to serve your loved ones and friends.

The latter is the picture of the servant's life. The idea of being a servant is foreign to many of us. The pervasive mind-set today is to be served rather than serve. But a servant, in the truest sense of the word, submits herself to someone else, expecting nothing in return. In the same way, you were put here on earth to be a blessing to others. God spoke some very powerful words to the prophet

Jeremiah: "Before you were born, I set you apart for a special work" (Jeremiah 1:5 NCV). That "special work" the Bible refers to is not just for paid professionals, such as preachers, pastors, and missionaries. Everyone who calls herself a believer in Jesus Christ is called to minister and to serve others.

When you serve others, you are actually demonstrating that you are grateful for what God has done in your life. Being a blessing to others is a response to the fact that you have been blessed. As you give of yourself, you are reminded that you have been given so much. Every daughter of the King knows that if she wants to be great in God's kingdom, she must be a servant. Great acts of kindness are not always necessary. It doesn't matter if anyone admires or acknowledges your act of kindness or even seems to care. God sees and cares about the work you are doing.

What are some practical ways you can serve someone today?

My Proclamation: I am a servant of Christ. I am blessed, and I am a blessing. People may not notice the acts of kindness I perform, but God takes notice. Serving people means serving Christ.

Dear Heavenly Father, what a privilege it is to serve You by serving others. Please forgive me for seeking to be served rather than serve. Make me a small part of Your great big cycle of giving, for when I am serving, I am most like You. In Jesus' name, Amen.

My Authority:
What I Can Do
Through Christ

$\mathcal{Day}$ 15

Interruptions

I will not be moved.

We can make our plans, / but the LORD determines our steps. (Proverbs 16:9 NLT)

If you're like the average woman, you keep a daily schedule. You have places to go and things to do, but plans are often interrupted, aren't they? Jesus never seemed to have a problem with interruptions. During His three-and-a-half-year ministry on earth, His daily life seemed to consist of one interruption after another as He attended to the constant needs of people. Like so many of us, Jesus was a busy person, with many demands on His life. Yet He was never flustered, bothered, or out of sorts due to these constant demands.

Consider the events of Matthew 9. The chapter opens with Jesus being interrupted and asked to heal a paralyzed man. He healed the man and continued on, only to be interrupted by accusations of blasphemy from the Pharisees. As He turned their accusations into a teachable moment, he was interrupted with an urgent request—a man's daughter had died, and he pleaded for Jesus to come to his home to raise her up from her deathbed. As Jesus and His disciples followed the man home, He was interrupted again by the woman with the issue of blood who touched the hem of Jesus' garment and was healed. Before the chapter closes, Jesus is interrupted several more times to give Himself away to others in need. Whew!

How did Jesus deal with the constant barrage of interruptions and gain clarity to say yes to some and no to others? Jesus demonstrates that we must look at life from an eternal perspective. "So be careful how you act; these are difficult days. Don't be fools; be wise: make the most of every opportunity you have for doing good" (Ephesians 5:15-16 TLB). Before each day begins, ask the Lord for His guidance concerning your agenda, your calendar, or personal events. Simply ask Him to guide you and help you accomplish His will for your day. Even ask for His help to address those interruptions that are sure to come— that you would see them as opportunities to be caught off guard by God's blessings and respond to them with grace and patience.

My Proclamation: God gives me wisdom, courage, and ability at all times. Therefore, I am able to accomplish all my goals. My heart is settled. My mind is stable. And my feet do not stumble because God orders my steps. I am on mission for Him.

Dear Heavenly Father, I know that interruptions happen. Some of them are bothersome, while some are opportunities—even blessings—from You. When they come, give me the grace and wisdom to know the difference. In Jesus' name, Amen.

Fear is a spirit that will paralyze you,
but that crippling spirit is not from God.
As a daughter of the Most High King,
you always have powerful weapons
in your arsenal.

Day 16

Keeping Your Eyes on Jesus

I cannot be shaken.

For God hath not given us the spirit of fear; but of power, and of love, and of a sound mind.
(2 Timothy 1:7)

A storm can paralyze you with fear. When Jesus called Peter to step out of the boat into the Sea of Galilee, Peter's heart responded with faith. In that moment his confidence in Jesus was so full and strong that Peter got out of the boat, in the middle of a violent storm, and actually walked on water. But when he took his eyes off Jesus and considered his circumstances, his heart was consumed with fear. He felt the ferocious winds dashing around him and the torrential waves rolling under his feet and immediately began sinking into the dark, deep, depths of the stormy sea. (See Matthew 14:25-32.)

No doubt you've been consumed with the spirit of fear at some time in your life. One young wife and mother found herself overwhelmed with responsibilities of raising children and taking care of her sick husband. Fear began to fill her heart as she noticed the bills piling up and everyone's needs increasing. One day she realized she had a choice—she could be paralyzed by fear and go down with the ship, or she could put her faith in God and ask Him to take control. And that is what she did. She began using her God-given authority to pray for her husband's healing. She learned to manage the family's budget. She stopped letting fear control her life, and things started turning around for her and her family. She learned the power behind the promise of Proverbs 18:10: "The name of the LORD *is* a strong tower; / the righteous run to it and are safe" (NKJV).

While you can't always predict the coming storm, you can prepare for it. Don't let it shake you. Fear is a spirit that will paralyze you, but that crippling spirit is not from God. As a daughter of the Most High King, you always have powerful weapons in your arsenal. Fight back with prayer, praise, and thanksgiving, and take authority over fear. Keep your eyes on Him and magnify His name. He will become larger than your fears.

My Proclamation: I declare that I am courageous. Fear is an enemy to faith and a snare from Satan. God's peace is available to me at all times. I exchange fear for God's great power, His encompassing love, and His sound way of thinking.

Dear Heavenly Father, my heart is filled with assurance today as I approach Your throne. I am so grateful that You are my peace in the storm. Knowing You are with me assures me I can accomplish anything! In Jesus' name, Amen.

Day 17

For the Love of Family

I will not be swayed.

Choose you this day whom ye will serve . . . but as for me and my house, we will serve the LORD.
(Joshua 24:15)

As a songwriter, I love the stories of great composers, and as a mother, I love stories about courageous women. One woman whose life displayed a godly example for her talented children was Susanna Wesley. A mother to nineteen, Susanna was concerned about the spiritual welfare of all of her children. She was known to pack their home on Sunday nights with as many as two hundred neighbors who gathered to hear her preach the message of Jesus. All of her children were truly dedicated to the cause of Christ and carried their spiritual heritage into their adult lives. Her fifteenth child, John, became the founder of the Methodist movement, and Charles, her eighteenth child, composed some of the greatest hymns the church has ever sung.

Susanna was a woman who endured great hardship. She was left with the responsibility of raising her family and maintaining the family farm when her husband was put in debtors' prison. The family suffered from numerous sicknesses, and some of her children even died. They lost their home in a fire. But throughout all the difficult circumstances, Susanna Wesley practiced what she preached, never faltering in her faith.[3]

Known as the Mother of Methodism, Susanna Wesley embraced the same godly virtues that every mother must instill in her children. Neither the government, the school system, nor the media are responsible for teaching virtues to our children. Goodness, integrity, respect, honesty, kindness, and responsibility have to be taught in the classroom of your home. Someday, after you are long gone, your children, grandchildren, nieces, nephews, godchildren, or foster children will speak of you with fond memories. Hopefully, they will pay you the highest compliment that could be paid to a family matriarch— that you were a woman who was sold out to God and dedicated to family.

My Proclamation: I boldly confess that my entire family is blessed. I teach my children to stand strong for the cause of Christ. I instill godly virtues and values into the lives of my children and other children I may influence. I dare to leave a legacy of love and faith for generations to come.

Dear Heavenly Father, thank You for my family and for my precious children. They are a treasure to me. Help me not only to teach them with my words, but to be a godly example to them in all that I do. In Jesus' name, Amen.

Day 18

Success God's Way

I belong to Jesus, and I set my sights on things above.

*Blessed be the God and Father of our Lord
Jesus Christ, who hath blessed us with all
spiritual blessings in heavenly places in Christ.
(Ephesians 1:3)*

All around the world, in both small farm communities and large urban cities, people have a passionate drive to succeed. Oftentimes when we think of success and prosperity, we think of fame and popularity, owning a nice house and car, or money in the bank. Our culture determines success by accomplishments, awards, name recognition, and possessions. But there is a danger in the endless and relentless quest for fame and notoriety. Unfortunately, the headlines are filled with sad stories of those who have chased fame only to find their pursuit empty and meaningless. Across the span of time, some of the world's most famous people have secured an infamous place in history, having lost their lives in search of vain pursuits.

Regardless of the culture, what people really want out of life is significance. True joy and significance for every believer comes not in making a name for herself, but in making the name of Jesus famous on the earth.

As you assess your life today, don't define your success according to the world's standards. Don't let material things like a house, a car, or a job position determine if you're successful. You can be a success and have none of those things. As well, you can have all those things and be a complete failure. Don't compare yourself to others, obsessing over how they look or what they have accomplished. That will only distract you from your God-given assignment. The life of Jesus is your example. If you are reflecting Him and accomplishing His purpose for your life, then you are a huge success. Because success is not defined by what you have but by Who has you.

My Proclamation: I choose God's standard for success. I give Him all my gifts and talents and He blesses my work. I am a success because I belong to God and I am obedient and loyal to Him.

Dear Heavenly Father, in the past I have measured success by the accumulation of stuff and things. I humbly confess that I have been driven by greed and a lust for the world's empty desires instead of being drawn by the fullness of Your Spirit. Thank You so much for giving me the gifts and talents I possess. Help me to use those gifts and talents to make You look good on the earth. In Jesus' name, Amen.

If you are reflecting [Jesus] and
accomplishing His purpose for your life,
then you are a huge success.
Because success is not defined by what
you have but by Who has you.

Day 19

Heavenly Minded, Earthly Good

Earth is my mission,
and heaven is my destiny.

Are you tired? Worn out? Burned out on religion?
Come to me. Get away with me and you'll recover
your life. I'll show you how to take a real rest. Walk
with me and work with me—watch how I do it.
Learn the unforced rhythms of grace. I won't lay
anything heavy or ill-fitting on you. Keep company
with me and you'll learn to live freely and lightly.
(Matthew 11:28-30 The Message)

Lori is a young lady whose life was changed by the power of God. Lori had been living with her abusive boyfriend in a dead-end relationship for almost twenty years when a friend invited Lori to a gospel music concert where I was the special music guest. She was deeply moved by the music, and she heard testimonies from women who had been changed by encounters with Christ. That night, at the conclusion of the event, Lori gave her heart to Christ. Then she bravely went home and told her boyfriend to pack his things and move out. She told him what she had experienced at the church that night, and how, for the first time, she knew God loved her. She knew she was cherished, forgiven, and accepted by God.

The same power that changed Lori's life is available to you too. Jesus invites you to live a life where you are not simply tolerated, but celebrated. You don't have to settle for stale crumbs that have fallen to the floor when you can take your place as an invited guest at the Master's banquet table. Jesus wants you to learn "the unforced rhythms of grace." That means to work in unison with Christ, realizing there is no striving in the work because Christ did the hard work on the cross. Your heart can be attuned to heaven while your feet are firmly planted on solid ground.

When you keep company with Jesus, you don't want to go back to the way things were. The empty things of earth pale in comparison to the promises of eternity. *Everything* changes when you have been with Jesus. You can release your stranglehold on the temporal things of earth and hold on to Christ as though your life depends on it. Because it does.

My Proclamation: God wants to help me. In obedience, I will let Him. As I walk in tandem with Jesus, I walk in His footsteps, shaking off the chains of the old life to put on a new life of total freedom in Christ.

Sweet Father, the closer I walk in Your footsteps, the more I desire to do Your will. Empower me to fulfill my calling here in the earth and not be tethered to the things of this world. I want to live my life Your way—freely and lightly. In Jesus' name, Amen.

Day 20

No Excuses

I declare that "I can do all things through Christ who strengthens me" (Philippians 4:13 NKJV).

The LORD had said to Abram, "Leave your native country, your relatives, and your father's family, and go to the land that I will show you. I will make you into a great nation. I will bless you and make you famous, and you will be a blessing to others. I will bless those who bless you and curse those who treat you with contempt. All the families on earth will be blessed through you." (Genesis 12:1–3 NLT)

When Abram ventured into the land of the unknown with his wife, Sarai, it cost him everything—family and friends and all that was familiar. They had no idea what lay ahead, but Abram and Sarai chose to venture into the unfamiliar with God rather than stay in a familiar place without Him.

No matter how daunting the task, if God calls you to it, He will help you to do it. You might be facing a task that seems intimidating, but rest assured that as you step out in faith, He will equip you for the challenge. Take your eyes off of yourself and your personal problems and focus on God's promises.

There was plenty of opportunity for Abram to shrink back in fear and miss out on God's great purpose, not only for him, but for future generations. Without knowing what was ahead, without knowing all that he would need, Abram stepped out, believing God would provide. When Abram packed up all his belongings and headed out toward Canaan, one thing he didn't take with him was excuses.

Do any of these sound familiar?

"I'm not the right age."

"I don't have the right kind of experience."

"I don't have the right resources."

"I won't fit in."

"I'm not qualified."

It doesn't matter what your story is. God can use anyone, in any circumstance. God doesn't call the qualified— He qualifies the called. When you can't, God can.

My Proclamation: It is God who calls, equips, and qualifies me. Excuses do not enter my mind or exit my mouth. I accept God's purpose for me with joy, and I envision the journey as a faith adventure, remembering if God calls me to it, He will help me to do it.

Gracious Father, thank You for allowing me to play an exciting role in bringing about Your purpose! My part may seem small, but I can do something significant that brings Your name glory. Help me to step out in faith, leaving behind the familiar, if that is where You are leading. Wherever You are is where the adventure is! In Jesus' name, Amen.

The moment you come to the end of yourself in your weakness is the very moment you arrive at the beginning of God in His strength.

Day 21

God Can Still Use You

All things are possible. So if God is for me, who can be against me?

I am glad to boast about my weaknesses, so that the power of Christ can work through me. That's why I take pleasure in my weaknesses, and in the insults, hardships, persecutions, and troubles that I suffer for Christ. For when I am weak, then I am strong.
(2 Corinthians 12:9-10 NLT)

God can use the most ordinary people to do the most extraordinary things. Each of us possesses God-given ideas, solutions, creations, masterpieces, and inventions. But because of fear, many people never discover those gifts and talents.

Have you ever talked yourself out of trying something new before you even attempted it? We allow our personal weaknesses to convince us that we are unusable, but in actuality, the moment you come to the end of yourself in your weakness is the very moment you arrive at the beginning of God in His strength. Don't shy away from new opportunities. Seize them. Don't run from the challenge—run to it. Regardless of your weaknesses, God can still use you to accomplish His purposes. Over and over again, the Bible tells how God used people with weaknesses to demonstrate His great strength.

Moses stuttered.

David was an adulterer.

Jacob was a trickster.

Rahab was a prostitute.

Abraham was old.

Sarah was cynical.

Naman was a leper.

Jehoshaphat was outnumbered

Peter was known to be impulsive.

Matthew was said to occasionally dip into the treasury.

Mary was a teenage mother.

Thomas was a doubter.

Mary and Martha were impatient.

And Lazarus was dead.

Every one of these people had obvious weaknesses, but God used them anyway! Really, God used them not in spite of their weaknesses but *because* of their weaknesses. When the miracle was completed, there was no question that God did it and that He was the One Who still deserves the credit.

Will you surrender your weaknesses so God can demonstrate His miraculous strength through you?

My Proclamation: I am inspired, resourceful, and creative! I open my heart and mind to new ideas and opportunities, no matter how challenging, knowing that even if I fail, it is an opportunity for discovery, to put God's mighty power on display.

Awesome God, You are so amazing! With You, nothing slips between the cracks or falls off the radar. Thank You, Lord, for the gifts and talents You have given me. I present them to You all over again today, even the gifts that I'm not aware of. Stir up my gifts and bring the good stuff to the top! In Jesus' name, Amen.

My Possibility:

How I Can Face Each Day

with Christ

When thanks-living becomes a way of life, you'll be grateful for even the smallest blessings and will realize how good God has been to you.

Day 22

The Gift of God's Love

My faith is rooted and established in love.

Then Christ will make his home in your hearts as you trust in him. Your roots will grow down into God's love and keep you strong.
(Ephesians 3:17 NLT)

Do you enjoy receiving gifts? What girl doesn't? Whether the treasure is in a gift bag billowing with colorful tissue or in a small velvet box, we all get excited about being on the receiving end of gift-giving. But have you ever felt as though you didn't deserve a gift given to you? Maybe you responded, "You shouldn't have! I don't deserve it. Let me pay you for this." That attitude denies the giver the pleasure of giving because gifts are never deserved or earned—a gift is bestowed in love.

In the same way, salvation in Jesus Christ is the greatest gift of all. Ephesians 2:8-9 says, "For it is by grace you have been saved, through faith—and this is not from yourselves, it is the gift of God—not by works, so that no one can boast" (NIV). No matter how hard you try, there is no way you could ever be good enough to earn God's favor. Because Jesus paid the debt for sin at the cross, you don't get what you deserve. You get what Jesus deserves. The gift of God's love and favor is yours—no strings attached!

So what should your response be? Our mothers taught us two words when we were on the receiving end of any gift, great or small: *thank you.* Saying "thank you" is always the appropriate response. When *thanks-living* becomes a way of life, you'll be grateful for even the smallest blessings and will realize how good God has been to you.

Praise God! His love is the gift that keeps on giving!

My Proclamation: I am confident in the love God has for me. I do not take that love for granted. Thanks-living is my way of life. I am established and strong in my faith, knowing every blessing I have has been bestowed to me through Christ Jesus. I am grateful that God smiles on me.

Kind Father, I have grown weary trying to be good enough to earn Your love. I know all my efforts are empty and futile. So I relax, with a heart of thanks-living, and let You carry me. I know You've got me! In Jesus' name, Amen.

Day 23

Keep Moving

Nothing I have done, or ever will do, can diminish God's power that is working in me and for me.

Then some Jews . . . stoned Paul and dragged him out of town, thinking he was dead. But as the believers gathered around him, he got up and went back into the town. (Acts 14:19-20 NLT)

Paul and Barnabas's first missionary journey reads like an exciting adventure novel, filled with challenges, miracles, and extraordinary encounters. Acts 14 opens with a description of how effectively the men preached while on their mission. They "preached with such power that a great number of both Jews and Greeks became believers" (v. 1 NLT).

Acts 14:2, though, begins with the word *but*: "But the unbelieving Jews stirred up the Gentiles and poisoned their minds against the brethren" (NKJV). The "buts" of life can seem like temporary power failures, pulling the plug on all your efforts. When you hear the word *but*, you know instinctively that trouble is near. You've graduated with your degree, *but* you're left with a boatload of student debt. Your husband says he loves you, *but* he wants a divorce. You love your job, *but* the company is downsizing and you are in danger of being laid off.

So what do you do when the buts of life sneak up on your blind side, clobbering you like a linebacker on the football field? Let the Lord pull you up. Use the buts of life to your advantage! Remind yourself that you might be down, *but* you're not out. Recall a time when God rescued you in the past. What He did back then, He'll do again! Empowering His daughters is one of the things that God does best! Just as He empowered the Apostle Paul to get up and continue his mission, He will empower you to meet your challenges head-on. If life hits you below the belt and brings you down, remember, you don't have to stay down. With His help, God expects you to get back up and get going again. Not in your own strength, but in His.

My Proclamation: Whenever I meet an obstacle, I face it head-on, reminding myself that this too shall pass. The obstacle I face is not a setback, but a set up to my comeback.

Almighty Father, sometimes this faith journey is so . . . daily. I admit, the routine of falling down and getting back up again can sap me of strength. Spiritually speaking, I have skinned knees and bruised elbows to prove it. You know my struggle, though. I find comfort in knowing that I am not alone in my struggle. You will help me with every assignment. With thanks, Your Daughter.

Day 24

A Mind Makeover

**I have the mind of Christ on every matter.
I make sound decisions,
and I exercise good judgment.**

*Oh, the joys of those who . . . delight in the law of
the LORD, meditating on it day and night.*
(Psalm 1:1-2 NLT)

In the church my father pastored, it was a common practice during the worship service for many members to stand and give a word of testimony during the worship service and declare openly the victories Jesus allowed them to win. One sister declared with exuberance, "Jesus is a heart fixer and a mind regulator." Can you say amen to that? When you yield your life to Jesus, the Holy Spirit governs your mind, enabling you to think good thoughts and have a grateful attitude. How do you accomplish that? By practicing the presence of God.

Just as you must practice regularly to learn how to type on a keyboard or play a piano piece, in the same way, you practice God's presence by routinely meditating on His Word. If you can spend immense amounts of time worrying, imagining the worst thing that could happen, then you can spend just as much time meditating on God's Word, imagining a favorable outcome. It's a simple process. Practice God's presence by being aware of His promises.

The precepts of God's Word are meant to be applied. Read them. Recite them. Rehearse them. Remember them. When you hide God's Word in your heart by meditating on the Scriptures, you are reminding yourself of what you know to be true about God. When your back is against the wall and you need encouragement, the Holy Spirit will remind you of just what you need to know. When an undesirable thought comes into your mind, apprehend it and replace it with a wholesome thought based on God's Word. Whether you are facing a personal challenge, dealing with relationship difficulties, driving in bumper-to-bumper traffic, or taking a walk, meditating on God's promises will keep you uplifted, productive, and fruitful.

My Proclamation: God is the author of peace. I have the mind of Christ, and I am in perfect peace because I keep my mind on Him. I strengthen my faith by keeping my mind on what I know to be true about God.

Dear God, this world is so noisy! Negativity comes at me from all directions, trying to rob me of the contentment You give. Grant me the strength to resist the noise and remind me of Your promises. I surrender my hurried pace, my anxious heart, my impulsive tongue, and my cluttered mind. I exchange it all for Your peace. In Jesus' name, Amen.

$\mathcal{D}ay$ 25

Trusting in Jesus

I put my trust in God,
regardless of what comes against me.

*Trust in the LORD with all thine heart; and lean not
unto thine own understanding.*

*In all thy ways acknowledge him, and he shall direct
thy paths. (Proverbs 3:5-6)*

One of my favorite pastimes is sitting at the piano and
singing from the hymnal. Many of our most beloved hymns
are inspired by the composer's personal experiences, such
as the hymn "'Tis So Sweet to Trust in Jesus" by Louisa
Stead.

The story goes that Louisa, her husband, and young
daughter were enjoying a family picnic on the shore of a
Long Island beach when they heard a cry for help. A young
boy was in the water and in distress, and Louisa's husband
attempted to rescue him. Tragically, both drowned as
Louisa and her daughter looked on helplessly. With her
husband gone, Louisa found it difficult to provide for her
daughter. One day, when their resources were nearly gone,
she discovered a gift of money and a basket of food left on
their doorstep. Louisa later penned the words,

'Tis so sweet to trust in Jesus,
and to take him at his word;
just to rest upon his promise,
and to know, "Thus saith the Lord."

Jesus, Jesus, how I trust him!
How I've proved him o'er and o'er!
Jesus, Jesus, precious Jesus!
O for grace to trust him more![4]

Do you know what the verb *trust* means? It means to rely on; to depend on; to place in someone's care, charge, or custody.[5] It's not God's plan for us to hold on to the cares of this life, but to roll every care onto Him. Are you praying for a miracle that has yet to come? Keep trusting! Allow God to have the last word concerning your situation. In every tumultuous circumstance, God is with you. He is in you to strengthen you. He is round about you to guide you. He goes before you to assure your victory. He undergirds you to sustain you. When you look at things from this perspective, you can believe in and hope for the best.

My Proclamation: I boldly declare that I fully rely on God's care for me. I am victorious in every situation and an overcomer in all my circumstances. Therefore, I can never lose.

Precious Father, I admit I don't know the way. I can't even see the next step in front of me. But You know the way. Take my hand and put me on the right road. Thank You, Sweet Father. In Jesus' name, Amen.

It's not God's plan for us to hold on to the cares of this life, but to roll every care onto Him.

$\mathcal{D}ay$ 26

Living Now, Here

**And nothing will be able to separate
me from the love of God in
Christ Jesus our Lord.**

*I'm absolutely convinced that nothing—nothing
living or dead, angelic or demonic, today or
tomorrow, high or low, thinkable or unthinkable—
absolutely nothing can get between us and God's
love because of the way that Jesus our Master has
embraced us.*

(Romans 8:38-39 The Message)

We all know how it feels to be rejected. Maybe you were rejected by the other girls on the schoolyard playground. Maybe you've felt the sting of rejection because of your skin color. Maybe your boyfriend or your husband rejected you. Rejection cuts deep and opens the doors of your heart for feelings of insignificance, emptiness, and isolation to come in. To try and get a handle on those feelings, maybe you obsess about the way things should be, or wonder about the way things could be, creating a vicious cycle of negative thoughts.

Can I tell you something true? There is someone who will never reject you. His name is Jesus. With Him you are never an outsider. He goes out of His way to minister to the lost, the lonely, the sick, and the broken, and He will go out of His way to help you. It doesn't matter where you've been or how long you've stayed, His love goes all the way to the brink of despair to bring you back.

Obsessing over past mistakes only causes regret. Being consumed with future plans only causes worry and steals joy. Living in the *what could be* or *what should be* robs you of valuable time, leaving you unproductive—stuck in the middle of nowhere with an unresolved outlook on life. Instead of living nowhere, live *now, here*. Live with the constant awareness that God loves and accepts you.

My Proclamation: I boldly confess that I am the beloved daughter of God. It is Jesus who brings me into a right relationship with my heavenly Father. I stand on the promise that I am a friend of God and nothing can ever change that!

Heavenly Father, thank You for loving me with an everlasting love. Even before the beginning, You loved me and called me Your own. I praise Your name for the freedom I have. Because of Jesus, I will never be hopeless, helpless, troublesome, bothersome, or worrisome to You. I know I am welcomed in Your presence and nothing can stand in the way of Your love for me. In Jesus' name, Amen.

As daughters of the Most High King,
we don't place our hope in some
earthly chance or event.
Our hope rests firmly and securely
in the Lord Jesus Christ.

$\mathcal{D}ay$ 27

Keep Your Hopes Up

I eagerly await Christ's return.

Hope in the LORD! / *Be strong! Let your heart take courage! / Hope in the* LORD! *(Psalm 27:14 CEB)*

Has your soul ever been in a deep, dark pit? Have you ever visited the pit of despair or depression or loneliness? Maybe you can identify with some of the things that Joseph went through. His amazing story begins in Genesis 37. He was wronged by his brothers, carried away by slave traders to a land of pagan worshipers, and sold again as a slave to Potiphar, an Egyptian official who worked for Pharaoh. He was a foreigner accused of a crime he didn't commit—a crime worthy of death—and he spent years in prison because of it. Joseph's sad story has the perfect ingredients for country songs, reality television shows, and Hollywood movies. There were so many things that didn't go right for Joseph. Yet the God of hope was with Him.

Hope is not the luck of the draw, or positive thinking, or wishing upon a star. Biblical hope is much more than that. Hope in God is the confident expectation of good, based on our Father's perfect character and the integrity of His promises. Hope is trusting God for a favorable outcome. When you hope in God, you see yourself blessed, even when the rent is due. When you hope in the Lord, you see your body healed, even if there's no more the doctors can do. Because of godly hope, you can envision every need being provided for, even though your bank account is overdrawn and you are unemployed. As daughters of the Most High King, we don't place our hope in some earthly chance or event. Our hope rests firmly and securely in the Lord Jesus Christ.

It's easy to grow more and more anxious when you read today's headlines. There are so many things that fill our hearts with concern. But the Bible tells us that when we see these things happening, we are to look up. Our redemption is closer than ever before! It's time to quit shouting your problems while whispering your praises. Put your hope in the Lord!

My Proclamation: I have hope because I have faith. One cannot exist without the other. I choose to place my hope in the Lord! I have the confident expectation that my best days are still ahead of me.

Dear Father, You are always aware of every need. Fill my heart with a buoyant hope and a relentless joy that overflows into every area of my life. In spite of what's going on in the world around me, I will always believe for the best. My hope is in You! In Jesus' name, Amen.

Day 28

God Knows You

On that great day He will know me and call me by name.

"I knew you before I formed you in your mother's womb. / Before you were born I set you apart."
(Jeremiah 1:5 NLT)

All of us have so many unanswered questions about God and about life. But be encouraged! God knows all the answers just as well as He knows you! So, let me ask you a question: Can you be content with what you know and trust God with what you don't know?

Maybe you have questions about things that are out of your control. If you do, allow me to suggest something that has given me comfort in those times.

First, know that God can handle your questions. If you have them, ask them. But if He doesn't answer them in the way you'd like, remember He knows the reason why. It could be that you are not ready for the answer, the timing isn't favorable, or the situation may be too complex for your understanding. Whatever the reason, God knows what you need because He has always known you intimately.

Next, consider asking questions that have definitive answers. For example, instead of asking open-ended questions like: "Why me? Why this? Why now?" ask, "God, how can You use this situation to bring You glory? How can I use this circumstance to help someone else? What attribute of Your character do You wish to show me during this season?" Don't fret over what you don't know. Find confidence in what you do know.

There are so many things I don't know about God. On the other hand, the things that I do know, I am really confident of. That's why I wrote the song "This I Know For Sure":

> There is a God is in Heaven
> And I am in His plan
> He will forsake me never
> My life is in His hands
> His boundless love will lead me
> As long as time endures
> This I know, this I know for sure[6]

When you give God your life, nothing can come between you and God's great plan for you. Not people. Not things. Not even hell itself can keep God's great plan for you from coming to pass. And if you know Jesus, the One Who has given you all these promises and more, then you know all you really, truly need to know.

My Proclamation: God knows everything. Therefore, I trust Him with my future. I have no reason to fear the days ahead. God is already there.

Dear Father, You know the questions I have even before I do, so I relinquish all concerns to You. I rest in Your love and care right now. Give me peace when I don't know the way. In Jesus' name, Amen.

As long as there is life and breath
in your body, you have the call from
Christ to keep putting love, in all
of its glory, on display.

Day 29

Flying Colors

His banner over me is love.

*He escorts me to the banquet hall; / it's obvious how
much he loves me. (Song of Solomon 2:4 NLT)*

For centuries flags and banners have been used as
symbols of pride and patriotism. We see them hoisted high
on government buildings, castles, ships, and churches,
displaying beautiful colors, national flowers, birds, and
crests. Do you know which flag represents the kingdom
of God? Love. Love is the banner that flies high over the
citadel of your heart. Love represents an immortal King
and an unshakable Kingdom that is dedicated to the cause
of Christ. Why must love fly so high over the castle of your
heart? Because the King presides there.

Your love relationship with God is alive and active. You
must nurture this relationship, keeping it fresh and pure.
Don't allow anger, malice, envy, or bitterness to taint or
hinder the flow of God's love in your life. When you keep
short accounts with God and people, you allow God's love
to be the thing that people see and admire about you. As
long as there is life and breath in your body, you have the

call from Christ to keep putting love, in all of its glory, on display.

So how should you best represent God's kingdom in the earth? First, stay connected to God's promises. Keeping God's Word in your heart will empower you to put God's love on display. Long after you've finished this book, continue this spiritual discipline in the days ahead. Next, stay committed to God's people. Continue to gather with other believers on a regular basis so you can maintain your passionate faith. Third, stay concentrated on God's purpose. Exercise the gifts God has given you. You were not created just to live a drab existence—you were meant to leave your colorful mark on the world!

My Proclamation: I will put God's love on display today so all will know where my allegiance lies. There is nothing about this world that is worthy of my loyalty. I am on God's side. I am a member of His family and a citizen of His royal Kingdom.

Dear Father, I am humbled that You personally escort me to Your banquet hall. Who could refuse an invitation so lovely as that? Today I accept Your invitation! I put my love for You on display, with passion in my heart. Let there be no mistake about it—my heart belongs to You, my Lord, my King, my All! In Jesus' name, Amen.

$\mathcal{D}ay$ 30

Dressing the Part

And I lift my voice in loudest hallelujahs to sing His praises forevermore.

To appoint unto them that mourn in Zion, to give unto them beauty for ashes, the oil of joy for mourning, the garment of praise for the spirit of heaviness; that they might be called trees of righteousness, the planting of the LORD, that he might be glorified.
(Isaiah 61:3)

One of my consistent prayers is that God would use me however and whenever He wants—both on stage and off. One day He took me up on that request as I was in the doctor's office, waiting to get a mammogram. I had just put on that paper-thin gown they gave me to wear when I heard a soft knock at the door. A nurse poked her head into the room. "Are you Babbie Mason?" she asked. "I knew that was you! I saw you at a Women of Faith Conference. Would you mind singing my favorite song, 'Amazing Grace'? Sing it the way you would in your preacher-dad's church!"

Before I could answer, she was already inviting coworkers into the room. Quickly, I literally tried to pull it together—I adjusted the paper-towel gown around me a little more securely, though it had no more to give. I, on the other hand, was about to give the concert of a lifetime. In a room full of nurses and technicians and the Lord knows who else, I sang at the top of my lungs,

> Amazing grace, how sweet the sound
> That saved a wretch like me…[7]

An examining room became a sanctuary. A paper-towel gown became a choir robe. Strangers became friends and fellow worshipers as I sang praises to God, encouraging the hearts of women along life's journey.

Are you cloaked in the spirit of heaviness today? Exchange those tattered rags for some new clothes! Adorn yourself with praiseworthy garments that celebrate your royal heritage. The garment of praise is the most beautiful garment the daughter of the Most High King can wear.

My Proclamation: I confess that life is a joyful journey, so I will revel in the ride! I have an attitude of gratitude because God loves me. Everyone I encounter today will be impacted by the zeal I have for the Lord and for life.

Gracious Father, nothing and no one can compare to You. Your loving-kindness and tender mercies are beyond description. I don't have enough words to tell you how much I love You. So I say "I love You" with my life. I am so glad to be the daughter of the Most High King! In Jesus' name, Amen.

Notes

1. *Merriam-Webster Online*, s.v. "so," http://www
   .merriam-webster.com/dictionary/so (accessed
   December 4, 2015).

2. http://mothertheresasayings.com/sayings.htm (accessed
   December 19, 2015).

3. *Faith Lift*, Babbie Mason (Lakeland, FL: Charisma
   House, 2003), 134.

4. "History of Hymns: 'Tis So Sweet to Trust in Jesus,'" C.
   Michael Hawn, Discipleship Ministries, http://www.
   umcdiscipleship.org/resources/history-of-hymns
   -tis-so-sweet-to-trust-in-Jesus (accessed December 19,
   2015).

5. *Trust, Merriam-Webster's Collegiate Dictionary*, Tenth
   Edition (Springfield, MA: Merriam-Webster, Inc., 1993),
   1269.

6. "This I Know for Sure." Words and music by Babbie
   Mason. Copyright © 2011 Praise And Worship Works.
   All rights administered by BMG Rights Management
   (US) LLC. All rights reserved. Used by permission.
   Reprinted with permission of Hal Leonard Corporation.

7. "Amazing Grace," John Newton, 1779.